A SIMPLE GUIDE TO

THE GOAT'S DIGESTIVE

SYSTEM

Series: Goat Knowledge 3

Felicity McCullough

Paperback Edition

My Lap Shop Publishers

Plymouth, England

www.mylapshop.com

Published by:

My Lap Shop Publishers

91 Mayflower Street, Unit 222,

Plymouth, Devon, PL1 1SB

United Kingdom

Tel: +44 (0)871 560 5297

www.mylapshop.com

www.goatlapshop.com

First Edition March 2012

ISBN: 978-1-78165-025-7

Copyright 2012 My Lap Shop Publishers

All Rights Reserved

Acknowledgements

The publisher thanks Danielle Shurskis for her support and help in bringing these series of books and articles to publication.

Disclaimer

This book is meant to be STRICTLY AN EDUCATIONAL AND INFORMATIONAL TOOL ONLY. The suggestions contained in this material might not be suitable for everyone. It is not intended to provide diagnosis or treatment. The author obtained the information from sources believed to be reliable and from personal experience. Although the best effort was made by the author, there are no guarantees as to the accuracy or completeness of the contents within this work.

The author does not guarantee the accuracy of any information or content in resources or websites listed or cited within this work. Additionally, the author, publisher and distributors never give medical, legal, accounting or any other type of professional advice. The reader must always seek those services from competent professionals that can review the particular circumstances. Mention of any product, brand or website is NOT an endorsement or recommendation of that product, service or usage.

The medical field is a very dynamic field that is constantly undergoing research, modifications and advancements and therefore information contained in this book should always be researched further and A VETERINARIAN OR OTHER SPECIALIST SHOULD BE CONSULTED where appropriate.

Any and all application of the information contained in this book is of the sole responsibility of the person performing said action. The author, publisher and distributors particularly disclaim any liability, loss, or risk taken by individuals who directly or indirectly act on the information herein. All readers must accept full responsibility for their use of this material.

Table of Contents

Introduction

The goat is a ruminant. What does this mean? Well, it basically means that animals in this category have a unique digestive system where their stomach has four compartments. Many times these animals are described as having four stomachs.

The aim of this guide is to provide information on the digestive system of ruminants, so that you can become more knowledgeable to improve the production of your animals.

As a goat keeper you need to understand what takes place in the goat's digestive system, so that you can optimise your goat's diet, to produce desired production, without causing unexpected and negative results.

It is not possible for goats to produce and produce well, without the proper diet.

Diet is also roughly 75% of the cost of raising goats.

Animal Classification:

According to Type of Digestive System

Animals can be classified according to the type of digestive system they have:

Monogastric

Monogastric animals have only one stomach. We are monogastrics, as is the horse, dog, cat and pig, just to name a few animals.

Hind-Gut Fermentors

These are animals that have only one stomach, albeit still have the capabilities of living off a highly fibrous diet. They are capable of digesting fibre because their large intestines are highly developed for it.

Polygastric

These animals are the ruminants that have the multiple stomachs or, in better terms, the four compartments to their stomachs.

This is an important classification because the monogastric animal is basically the opposite of the polygastric animal in terms of what they eat.

Polygastric animals or ruminants require a diet based on vegetation, whereas monogastrics require foods that are more easily digestible.

According to Diet

Animals are also classified, in terms of diet as herbivores, carnivores or omnivores.

Herbivores

Herbivores are animals that eat mostly plants and vegetations. Ruminants fall into this category. There are actually two different kinds of herbivores: the browser and the grazer.

Browsers

These are animals that are choosy eaters and will aim for the most easily digestible plants. These plants are high in starch, proteins and fats.

Browsers are less capable of digesting plants with high levels of fibrous material, like cellulose.

An example of this type of eater is the white-tailed deer.

Grazers

Grazers are animals that have the ability to eat a more fibrous diet. Their digestive systems have a more developed fermentation system. Because the plants they eat are tougher to digest and are usually lower in nutrients, they require a greater amount. That is why they are almost always eating.

The goat is called a browser, yet actually falls in between these two types. Preferentially goats will choose the best, most nutritious parts of the plants, which are what browsers do and yet are capable of eating very fibrous, tough plants, which is a characteristic of the grazer.

Carnivores

These are animals that eat meat. Dogs, cats and other predators that are a danger to ruminants fall under this category.

Omnivores

Omnivores are animals that eat both meat and plants. We are omnivores and so are rats and pigs.

Anatomy: The Ruminant Stomach

The ruminant's stomach is divided into four sections: the reticulum, the rumen, the omasum and the abomasum.

The Reticulum

The first and second sections of the ruminant stomach are often referred to together as the reticulo-rumen, because they work intimately together.

Another name for the reticulum is the honeycomb, because of how it looks.

The main purpose of the reticulum seems to be as a sort of filter. It makes sure that only small particles pass on to the omasum.

The reticulum also participates in the process of regurgitation, or cud chewing and the expelling of gases.

There are a lot of micro-organisms present and fermentation also occurs here.

In cattle, there is a tendency for foreign objects to get stuck here, which causes the infamous Hardware Disease. This is a less common occurrence for goats.

The Rumen

The second compartment, the rumen, is arguably the most important compartment of the stomach. Its nickname is the Ponch.

The Rumen is the largest part of the digestive system. It is located on the animal's left side.

What happens in here is also one of the most complex processes and is based on biochemistry. Experts spend years of study just on this alone and while this level of knowledge is not necessary, of course, it is essential that at least the basis of what goes on in the rumen is understood.

The rumen is an anaerobic environment that houses billions of microorganisms including bacteria, yeast, protozoa and fungi. It is estimated that there are around 10 to 50 billion bacteria and 1 million protozoa, yeast and fungi in each millilitre of rumen contents! That's a lot of micro-organisms!

These micro-organisms participate in the breakdown of the ingested food through fermentation. Many things happen during this process, including the production of by products and volatile fatty acids.

Volatile fatty acids are what the ruminant uses for energy.

All along the walls of the rumen are located papillae; these are projections out of the wall, which are responsible for the absorption of the volatile fatty acids produced, as well as other nutrients.

The Omasum

The third section of the ruminant stomach is the omasum, also called the Piles or the Butcher's Bible, because it looks like it is covered in folds or leaves of a book.

There is less known about this section of the stomach. It is believed to participate in the grinding of food particles and the absorption of water.

The Abomasum

The nickname of the third compartment is the "true stomach". It is the part that is similar to our stomachs. It produces the stomach acids that aide in the digestion of the particles that are able to get through the rumen.

The Abomasum is where internal parasites such as Barber Pole Worms and other stomach worms attack.

The Young Ruminant

The baby ruminant is born with all the sections of the digestive system, but at birth the rumen is not functional. The rumen develops later, when it is exposed to solid foods.

The rumen develops more quickly when the kid is fed with grains rather than with forage.

Creep Feeding

Creep feeding young ruminants is so important to help develop the rumen and wean from its dam (mother).

You want to offer free access to highly digestible feed, such as cracked corn.

The young animals should be allowed to eat as much as they want. They usually do not overeat. The important thing is to always keep grain in the creep feeder. The problem comes when it runs out and then is refilled, as the animals miss it and then might overeat.

Vaccinations

These animals should also be vaccinated for overeating disease, which is caused mostly by *Clostridium perfringens* type D.

Pregnant does (female goats) should be vaccinated about a month before kidding.

After the kid drinks the colostrum, shortly after birth, they will be protected for about 6 weeks through the vaccination given to the dam. After this time, they should be vaccinated directly and then a booster given roughly 4 weeks later.

Esophageal Groove Reflex

The abomasum is designed to digest milk.

Ruminants have a reflex called the Esophageal Groove Reflex, or Ventricular Groove that is activated when they suckle. It creates a kind of tube that permits the milk to bypass the rumen and fall directly into the abomasum.

Tube Feeding

Tube feeding kids does not elicit the Esophageal Groove reflex, meaning that milk is deposited into the rumen, which is then fermented. This can cause diarrhoea.

Drenching

Esophageal Groove Reflex can actually cause some problems later in life.

An adult ruminant has this reflex and it can be activated by drenching. When this happens the medicine is deposited into the abomasum instead of the rumen.

In order to avoid the drenching going direct into the abomasum, the medicine should be deposited directly into the oesophagus and over the "hill" of the tongue.

Feed Trajectory

The digestive system consists of the mouth, oesophagus, reticulum, rumen, omasum, abomasum, small intestines, large intestines, and anus. The food that the animal eats will pass through all of these parts after it is eaten.

Rumen Biochemistry Basics

Food enters the mouth, where it is chewed and mixed with saliva. After swallowing, it will go into the reticulorumen complex where it will be exposed to the microorganisms, which will begin the fermentation process.

pH

The rumen, as stated earlier, is basically an anaerobic fermentation vat.

The pH should be maintained at around 6 or 7. This is fundamental for the health of the goat. If the rumen becomes too acidic, it will cause problems.

Layers in the Rumen

The contents of the rumen naturally form into three layers: a liquid layer at the bottom, a more solid layer of fibrous material in the middle and a gas layer at the top. The rumen suffers contractions, which will move these layers and mix them up periodically.

Chewing the Cud

The function of the reticulum, as stated earlier, is to prevent large particles of food moving through to the omasum. It does this by redirecting these particles back up into the mouth for re-chewing.

When ruminants do this, it's called chewing the cud.

Eructation

During the fermentation process, there is a lot going on biochemically, including the production of gases. These gases must be released somehow and the ruminant does this through eructation, which results in belching.

Rumen Population

The rumen is filled with different types of microorganisms. The diet affects this population of microorganisms in different ways. The population is also affected by pH levels.

Micro-organisms

Primary bacteria are bacteria that break down nutrients and feed particles directly.

Secondary bacteria are microbes that break down the product of the primary bacteria. These bacteria produce energy for the goat. They also synthesize vitamins; especially important are vitamin K and the B-complex vitamins.

The bacteria themselves can pass on to the rest of the digestive system and provide a source of protein for the goat. Bacteria also can convert non-protein nitrogen into protein. This is why cows are fed urea, which is a source of nitrogen.

Volatile Fatty Acids

80% of the goat's energy comes from the volatile fatty acids that the microbes of the rumen produce. Volatile fatty acids are absorbed by the papillae in the rumen.

There are different types of volatile fatty acids in existence. The three most important for the ruminant are acetic acid, propionic acid and butyric acid and these range from highest production to lowest.

Acetic Acid

Acetic acid is produced normally in the highest proportion at 50% to 60%. It takes part in the synthesis of fat and, consequently, is very important in milk production, as it is responsible for the production of butterfat. It is produced in greater proportion in diets rich in forage.

Giving a lot of forage is the most natural of diets. The goat chews a lot and food takes longer to pass through the system and the pH goes up.

What makes ruminants so special is their ability to digest the cellulose in plants. They are able to do this because of the microbes in the rumen.

When you feed a diet high in forage, the bacteria that digest cellulose predominates, and they produce mostly acetate, which is also called acetic acid.

Propionic Acid

Propionic acid is the second most abundant volatile fatty acid produced, with levels normally within the 18% to 20% mark. It is very important because it is converted to glucose, which in essence is pure energy.

Often it is a goal to increase levels of this volatile fatty acid to increase production. This is done through the use of Ionophors such as Bovatec® or Rumensin®.

If you raise the levels of proprionic acid, you will correspondingly decrease the levels of acetic acid.

Ruminants are capable of being fed a high concentrate diet, such as corn and other grains.

Microorganisms that break down starches are favoured with this diet and they produce more proprionic acid.

This diet causes less chewing and production of saliva and the feed passes more quickly through the system.

The pH also drops due to the production of lactic acid.

Too much concentrated feeds will cause grain overload or acidosis. This is a potentially fatal condition where the rumen pH drops too much.

Butyric Acid

Butyric acid is usually in the 12% to 18% range and is metabolised and oxidised into ketones. It provides energy to the rumen and its wall and therefore energy increases with high grain feed.

What you are trying for is a balance between these three volatile fatty acids. They each are important and have their functions. For instance, you cannot produce milk without both propionic and acetic acids. More propionic acid means more milk is produced, yet acetic acid is important for butterfat. You cannot increase the levels of propionic acid, without correspondingly decreasing the amount of acetic acid.

Protein Metabolism

There are two types of protein. One that is metabolised in the rumen and the other that is able to pass through the rumen.

Degradable Intake Protein

This type of protein gets into the rumen. Then the microbes present in the rumen, breaks it down in ammonia, amino acids and peptides. Some of the microbes do pass on to the abomasum and are used by the goat as a source of protein.

Undegradable Intake Protein or Bypass Protein

This type of protein is also known as Protected Protein and Escape Protein. It is somehow protected from the microorganisms. There are many ways that this can be done. The details go beyond this work. What is important is that this protein gets past the rumen and into the abomasum. It is then absorbed.

Traditionally, this feed was animal protein. Ever since the problems with Mad Cow Disease, though, it is illegal to feed certain types of animal protein to ruminants. You are permitted to feed fish meal and feather meal still.

Some other sources of protein are soybean meal, distiller's grains and co-products left over after the production of ethanol.

Chewing Cud and Eructation

Chewing cud is the act of regurgitating the food to be chewed and broken down into smaller particles.

One of the things that a veterinarian will look at when examining ruminants and ruminant herds is the percentage of the herd, or the percentage of time that the ruminant spends chewing cud.

Goats usually spend a considerable amount of time chewing cud.

Bloat

Gases produced during fermentation are gotten rid of through eructation or belching. If something happens and gases accumulate, this is called bloat and it can be potentially fatal. There are different kinds of bloat.

Carbon Dioxide and Methane Gases

The two gases produced the most are carbon dioxide and methane gas. Methane is a greenhouse gas and the reason why ruminants get some bad press. It is estimated that roughly 28% of these gases come from ruminants.

There are several methods that can be taken that reduce the production of methane.

These include: -

- A diet with higher digestibility, improving animal productivity;

- Ionophors, such as Rumensin® and Bovatec®;

- Microbials found in essential oils and plant extracts;

- protected nutrients;

- Buffers such as sodium bicarbonate; and

- feed additives, such as tannins.

Some countries have even instituted a Flatulent Tax or 'Fart Tax' in the hopes of reducing methane.

Australia has developed a vaccine that reduced methane discharge from animals.

De-Wormers

Currently de-worming medicines can have big problems with resistance to worms. Check with your veterinarian to ensure your de-wormers are giving your goats the best protection, as well as having a good system for regular testing and being observant.

Fasting is recommended before drenching, because this slows the digestive processes down giving the drenching medicine more time to work.

Important Things to Keep in Mind

Always make any dietary changes gradually over a couple of weeks. The populations of microbes in the rumen need time to adjust.

Feed a well-balanced diet based on forage with enough concentrate, or grains to meet the goat's needs.

Your feed requirements will differ and is dependant on your productivity needs from your goats. Output will be determined by economics to optimise produce and or meat growth.

With well balanced rations, your aim will be to increase productivity resulting in the need to keep and feed fewer animals.

Resources

Goat Basics www.goatlapshop.com

Articles and Other Goat Books by Felicity McCullough in the series at:

www.goatlapshop.com:

Boar Goats (article)

Charlie And Isabella's Magical Adventure (book)

Charlie And Isabella Meet Jacob (book)

Charlie And Isabella's Second Adventure With Jacob (book)

Charlie And Isabella's Magical Adventures Compendium (book)

Diseases of Goats (article)

How To Keep Goats Healthy (article)

Nigerian Dwarf Goats (article)

Nimbkar Boer Goat (article)

The Fun of Goats (article)

About Felicity M<u>c</u>Cullough

Felicity McCullough has written several books about preventative health care for goats.

The website dedicated to goats www.goatlapshop.com has a wide variety of topics and resources that relate to goats, including the Charlie And Isabella's Magical Adventures Series of Children's Books, suitable for bed-time reading that are beautifully illustrated.

www.ingramcontent.com/pod-product-compliance
Lightning Source LLC
Chambersburg PA
CBHW070931270326
41927CB00011B/2818